The Way I Feel It

The Way I Feel It

Tanyaradzwa Vimbai Mombeshora

Published by Tanyaradzwa Vimbai Mombeshora, 2024.

While every precaution has been taken in the preparation of this book, the publisher assumes no responsibility for errors or omissions, or for damages resulting from the use of the information contained herein.

THE WAY I FEEL IT

First edition. July 8, 2024.

ISBN: 979-8227301796

Written by Tanyaradzwa Vimbai Mombeshora.

Table of Contents

# Tanyaradzwa Mombeshora

Words

Each letter formatted together in a
Graceful written design,
Or perhaps the most beautiful uttered sounds
Put together they create words like particles
Of the atmosphere we cannot live without,
Like the very air we breathe
We learn , depend, enjoy and live by them
We twist, bend , shake, exaggerate and
Manipulate them.
How we use the written word,
Perhaps the spoken word determines
Our way of life
For the divergent shakes them
To question society
The violent manipulates them to start a war
The peaceful uses them to end one
The lovers exaggerate them to describe emotions
The liar twists and bends them as a way out.
However you use them
Like dust lifted high up into a sandstorm
Or rain showering with blessed water
To quench a thirsty body for nothing more
Delightful has ever touched the tongue
They are like florescent light that
Shines brightly in a darkened world
Perhaps they can be the whirlwind
That darkens one

Not a word lost
Not a word forgotten
Forever remembered
Sometimes saved and some even stolen
The power of words

Prickly Bush Of Thorn

There is a prickly bush of thorns,
No good comes from it.
Most hated in the garden.
The sight of it is danger,
Touch it, it stings pain.
The prickly bush of thorns.
You long to dig it's roots out.
Cut it down.
Enough of bleeding fingertips.
Cussing each time you accidentally touch it.
No use at all.
Unimaginable should the children trip into it.
It grows there prickly bush of thorns.
So often it reminds me of myself.
Different altogether from other plants in the garden.
Aggressive in every way.
They long to remove it as they wish I would disappear.
It grows alone as I thrive alone.
Singular and strange.
One morning a stem of the prickly bush of thorns produces no plants.
None other than a stunning rose.

Tired

I fought the good fight,
Refusing to be silenced.
At each other's throat we went.
Punch after kick,
Pain with injuries.
Endless battles, ongoing war of life
I ran a great race.
Aiming for the finish line.
My body stronger than I knew,
Pushing limits unbelievable stamina,
I never knew I had it in me.
Pursuing devotedly to win winners reward of life.
Today I have fallen on the ground.
I am sick, sick and tired of trying to be,
Always working never gaining.
I despise that life is unfair ,
I am tired, tired of being strong solider.
I am tired, tired of being an unmatched runner.
I am tired, tired of being a spirited dancer.
I just want to cry
Shout and cry.
I am tired.

The Move

I pushed you away perhaps a bit too far.
My intentions were to make you forget.
I thought you would,
I hoped you could.
I was glad when you did.
Then it hit me.
You truly turned your back.
You moved on forward.
It hurt yet you pulled yourself together.
Strange thing how the heart works.
It was what I wanted I thought,
Yet after years you remain an obsessive memory.
I thought I moved before you did,
Yet here I am in the long last place I ever dreamt of.
Here I am trying to forget,
But something keeps pulling me back to the place I left you.
Except you are there no more.

Misunderstood

I replay events in my head.
Trying to comprehend what has occurred.
What just happened?
Why am I at war with the world?
I try to change,
Be better be different,
Here I am doing my best.
Taken for the worst.
Oh dear, I mean well.
Why can you not see that.
Always assuming the worst .
You never ask you always assume.

Kiss A Frog

Kiss a Frog till you find your prince they say.
I am the frog.
They kissed me all,
Gently lifted me from swamps with their bare hands.
Placed me on their palms.
Sheltered me from vultures and predators.
They took me all.
Loved me whole.
Closed their eyes as they delivered that kiss.
The magic kiss.
True love's kiss.
They held me in their palms.
With an open heart.
Hoping to see my slimy green skin peel away.
They looked me deep in the eyes.
Searching for her.
My heart always breaks for them.
I am not a princess,
I will never be your princess.
Alas, you have chosen a mere ugly frog.

Untitled

As I hang on to dreams like I hang onto a ripping rope,
I try to collect them as one collects dust.
Remember each wish as one remembers a season passed
Remain true to each prayer as one is true to their nature.
I labour for progress as one labours for harvest,
Fishing out results as one fishes out salmon.
Hoping dawn will break with a different result.

You Called Him Love

What did you name him when you first met?
One of the others who filled your head with
Endless empty vows of eternal love? Promising the moon?
No, he was different and you knew him by name.
Remembered his name for he made you laugh
You went to sleep blushing and restless.
You could not wait to see him again.
When you met the second time,
What was it that you called him?
In his company you felt like the only woman in the world.
Like Aphrodite or perhaps Venus.
Or maybe just you but lovelier.
You went home dreaming houses, jobs and babies.
You went home thinking I will never be lonely.
When I asked you yet again, 'what do you call him?'
You called him love.

Reflection

I look into the mirror and a stranger looks back.
She reminds me of someone I never want to know.
Someone I am afraid of knowing.
She is truth, vulnerable and love.
No I don't want to see her.
Into the mirror I punch my clutched fist.
I watch it crack then break.
Pieces of the young woman fall into a puzzle.
I do not attempt to rearrange it.
With my bleeding knuckles I walk away.
I never walk away.
I am always running away from that reflection.
Truth, vulnerability and love.
I never ask her who she is and what she needs.
She needs too much.
She will never have it.
So I put on an armor made of fire.
With eyes strong as steel.
I hide that woman from the world with a simple smile.
Ready to fight the battle of life
Fighting for a home where I will never belong.
For I do not know myself without my armour.

Missing You

I lived in a world of my own.
Peaceful, quietly and serenely.
Needed no one.
Lived alone, never felt lonely.
Then you came along.
Along you came.
I resisted, built walls so high
You could never climb them if you tried.
Tried you did.
You gave your all.
Till you finally left.

Now I sit alone feeling lonely.
I wish I let you in.
If I could say it all in a few words.
They would be ,
' I miss you.'

Untitled

I hit ground hard.
Numb to the pain of violent fall.
What I feel is you.
You who never cares.
You who comes and goes.
Broken promises, lies and betrayal.
All I have ever known since I met you.
I promised myself l will forget you.
Picking up the pieces of my broken heart.
Mending it like I am putting a puzzle together.
I hate you I cry.
I hate you I laugh.
I hate you I scream.
Tomorrow you will knock on my door.
A pattern I have learnt since we met.
You apologize.
I forgive.
The following day I will cry once again for you.

If Only

I am at the front of your gate again.
Memories flood through my head,
My heart arches from the thought of you.
You who I let go of.
I stare at the front light og your porch.
If I could reach it,.if my feet could move towards it.
If only.
If only I had known better.
I think of how you made me laugh.
How you taught me love.
All we had, all we lost.
If I could walk towards the light,
To the light that keeps my beloved.
I miss u.

Sorry

I watch you go knowing there is no return.
Yet again another one goes.
To make you stay I need only utter one word.
Alas, I am to proud to say it.
I won't say it .
I can't say it.
I follow you to the door.
Silently tracing your steps.
You look back,
Hoping to see a sign.
Sign of regret,
Sign of hope,
Sign of change.
Regret is there, change is not.
So you walk out stepping into the darkness.
I fall on the doorstep.
Watching you disappear into the night.
I cry on my own.
I run not after you.
No, I won't follow.
No, I will not beg.
I am to proud, to proud to say SORRY.

Ghost

I thought you were long gone and buried.
I learnt to live without you,
I told myself.
I taught my heart to be without you,
I swore to myself.
Yet you keep returning,
Haunting me so.
The ghost of my past.
A past I cannot undo.

The Crush

Old habits die hard.
You were always mine to a fault,
A drug I could quit.
False promises never sounded more unbelievable.
I never fell for the words you say,
I fell hard for the games you played.
Crushing down hard in your playground.
You watch me fall without shame.

Attack

Your words stab my heart like a hundred daggers.
Sharp they come, deadly they are.
I fall to the ground.
Face down in the mud

Your words shoot my soul like a thousand bullets.
Loud as thunder they are released,
Speed so quick, so invincible they kill.
To the earth I rest and she swallows me whole.

Your words burn like a million types of poison.
I will not name them or count.
I listen, endure as my insides turn .
I cry out in anguish.
I struggle I scream I crawl.
When it is done I am glad.

Another Argument

You were complete till you met her.
You love her no doubt.
You understand her a little.
Oh dear, you try.
One moment it is this , the next it is that.
You were complete now you are puzzled.

She screams, you try to calm her storm.
She yells you are patronizing.
You watch silently.
She claims you do not listen.
You love her.
Heaven knows why she changes moods so quickly.
All you said was...Perhaps it was wise not to repeat.
So you apologize.
Why are you sorry? Who knows?
Just say sorry.
Lord knows, she is always right.
Umm.

The Vow

As you promised till death do us apart.
You stood tall, stood smiling.
You looked me in the eyes,
As you promised to forsake the others,
You rejoiced.
Today you stand hunchback.
Face falling to the floor,
My eyes you refuse to meet.
So this is love? You leave before my death.
So this is love? You swore to forsake them.
Bags packed, not a single smile
I was young, vigorous and pretty.
Now I am used up and mundane.
So you go, you go to her.
You do not rejoice as if I believe
It hurts you to hurt me.
As if you care for the heart you are breaking.
As if...

Untitled

The dark clouds rolling in,
No sign of rain this is no storm.
This is us, men we have crippled the air
Smoke here smoke there.
Burning this burning that. Chemicals.
Choke the world and us with it.
Ground dries up,
Drought claims fruitation.
Animals starved.
We survive science replaces nature.
Manufactured food to slowly poison the heart.
The heat tortures penguins.
Do you see the polar bears run?
The ice is melting their world to oblivion.
Oceans rising washing away the land.
They cry out the animals, ' You did this.'

What was once the most pure is now contaminated.
Could you drink it? Water?
Have you seen the dams, rives and lakes?
Rejected items fill them rubbish upon rubbish.
Fish suffocated, plagues created.
'The fish shout, ' You did this.'
' Aye,' I reply,' so we did.'

Untitled

I blink thrice adjusting my sight to the blinding light.
I have reached the Frozen peak,
I have conquered the mountain.
I bled,wounds, frostbites , fear,
Had it all.
The voices in my head planting doubt in my heart.
I smile I have made it.

I look forward to the other side ready to climb down.
Yet I will never forget the side I will leave behind.
Each rolling stone, crushing boulder, rough ground, piercing ice.
The pain I will carry,
Never forget it.
I smile to myself as I make my way down.
The unbearable part I defeated it.

The Sun and The Moon

He was the sun to your moon,
They saw you because of him.
In the night he stood behind
So you could be seen as stunning as you are.
But your star glows brighter in the presence of your burning star
Without him there is darkness,
Neverending coldness.
You needed his warmth to be remembered,
You needed his radiance to be seen.
You always borrowed his light.
The Sun is here no more.
Another moon he has found,
Brighter, kinder and prettier and now he has forgotten.
He burns for her and her glow is now seen by others.
The truth hurts and you know it.
He loves you no more,
Yet you won't let go.
You miss his radiance,
You need his warmth.
Moon wants her sun back,
She refuses to be forgotten.

Untitled

Where do dreams go?
Went to sleep so young full of hope and courage.
We dared to shape the world to our thoughts,
No stopping us the invincible.
To our despair we awoke as adults,
Full of doubt full of fear.
Confusion roams the mind like a lion.
Heartbroken we called our unfulfilled dreams fantasy.
I am certain if we turn back time,
Undo the mistakes,
We will take a chance and fulfill dreams.
We would chase them to the end of the world.

Innocent Eyes

I used to have them once,
Them innocent eyes.
Needed no rosy spectacles to make believe,
A more jovial world.
Loved the oceans and it's tumultuous waves.
Hurricanes even.
Such might of the wind.
Think about it,
From the magnificence of a gentle breeze,
To the almost fantastical world ending blows.
In its tragedy is its beauty.
Worth saving I used to say.

Everyone deserves another chance,
I used to believe.
I saw the change in my mind without owning rosy spectacles.
To work together creates a better.
What're the weather we are in this together.
Love one another I preached to others.
Alas, I am grown .
What life has done to me.
I used to have them once,
Them innocent pair.
I learnt the hard way throughout history from dawn of creation,
Till now and forever.
There is no unity.

Untitled

My heart skips a beat by the sight of you,
Eyes wide open,
Tongue dry and speechless.
An angel I see,
True vision of beauty
Beauty in its truest glory,
I am graced by your presence,
Dreaming of your attention,
A moment of your consideration,
Is worth the treasures of El Salvador.
A moment of your time is worth the world and more.
I am looking at you,
Hope you will notice.
Never have my eyes beheld such an exquisite creature .
Never will my heart know someone like you.

On My Door

One, two, three, four or was it seven?
I lost count of those who knocked on my door.
Seven, eight, nine or was it fourteen?
Who was it I locked out last month?
When they knocked on my door?
Here I am standing before my door awaiting a knock.
No one knocks.

I was warned once to let one in or I will be lonely.
Nothing is wrong with number thirteen,
Give him a chance for he loves you more than life.
But I was hard inside I knew nothing about love.
How to give it or receive it.
Now I find myself lying on the floor alone.
Knowing now the difference of being alone and being lonely.
Feeling the burden of a one-woman army.
Times as these I am in need of a general.
But I shut them all out.
One, two, three, four or was it seven?
Seven, eight, nine or was it fourteen?
It has been a month or two I count.
Zero knocking on my door.

Pick Yourself Up

Tis hard the game of survival.
One minute you journey a stable path,
The next moment you find yourself travelling
A road full of portholes.
Stumbling and tripping on the rocky roads.
Your feet bleed, your eyes are bruised from
After you fell on your face.
Face down covered in dirt and shame,
Cry as you may,
But don't stay on the ground.
Pick yourself up it is not the end.
It may feel like it is but it is never the end
Quite the challenge learning how to fly.
Even birds have to master their wings.
Feel the wind rush through their feathers,
They take a leap of faith.
Knowing death awaits them if they fail to fly.
Despite all odds they take off at first try.
It is in their nature to fly ,
Against their nature to be grounded.
So they take off and glide till they fly.
Do the same despite the voices.
Pick yourself up and glide till you fly.
For dreams are meant to be dreamt by those who dare.
Dare to hope dare to turn hope into faith.
For faith turns vision into motive for change,
Change becomes reality.

Reality never comes without opposition.
There will be battles you win and feats you will lose.
But of you are to win a war,
Pick yourself up and reach for your gun.
Aim at the obstacle and pull the trigger to kill the doubt.
Only when it is dying do will the bitterness and envy.
Now pick yourself up and move.

Lament

Victory yet to come
Joy shadowed with misery
Home yet to find
Clouds rolling in
Dawn yet to break
Sorrow overflows
Dreams yet to come true
Another broken soul.

In My Mind

She cries out to be saved like helpless little babe,
Hoping to be nursed of her ailments.
Her greatest fear was to become the unknown,
Maybe worse the unloved.
She was afraid no one will hear her speak so she cried.

She cries out loud when darkness comes with the night.
All have gone to bed so it is silent enough to hear without distraction.
She cries out for me to let her out so I can let others in.
I fight her to sleep till she sleeps with me,
Only to awaken with I as well.
Frustrated I ask,' Who are you?'
She replies,' I am you.'
For the first time I see the girl with the crying voice.
She was me before I was who I think I am.
Who l am trying to be.
Until I let her in I will never love another.
I see her clearly she is broken and scarred.
Bruised with life and it's unkindness.
I wished she wasn't I but she is.
Until I learn to love her I will never love another.
So I picked her up and carried her in my arms,
Nursed her illness and wrote her this poem.

The Sun

With darkness gone enters the light.
In the midst of childhood misery,
I always stood at the edge of the cliff.
Not to jump it never,
But I was waiting for the sun.
I went throught it all battles of life,
Dead dreams, broken hearts, endless fights
So I can be here.
A place where I am no longer safe but living.
I see the sun rise it's horizon painting
Grey skies purple and orange and I smile.
I feel the radiance and warmth kiss my skin.
I used to want closure to go back to a place where I felt safe.
Not anymore.
With dangers of life I have grown stronger
I have grown period and now I am proud
Of who I was and happy with who I am.
I walk away from the cliff where I was waiting for the sun.
The skies are blue and clear.
I hear the birds singing as I leave the past at the cliff.
Each lush green grass I step on promises life fulfilment,
There will be anger, sadness and disappointments but never bitterness.
For I am living under the sun.

Invincible

Dear old friend forgive me for letting you go.
One has to protect what is left of a broken heart.
Since childhood I learnt to stand alone,
I was silenced so I pen down what I cannot say.
I never know if I am loved for who I am or what I look like.
I found no comfort to be who I am outside of my mind,
So I hide away from all.
If I was invincible.
Unbreakable as a diamond,
Strong as superheroines I love to read in comics,
Unfeeling as a sinking stone,
I would give you all that I am.
If I was a dare devil who walked through fire,
Steady as a rock firm as waves crush over it.
Free as a bird that flies to the ends of the world,
I would love you with all that I am.
I am not invincible.
I bleed when pierced by a dagger.
When I fall to the ground I break into pieces.
Crushing into beautiful shattered glass pieces.
I am no wonder woman bulletproof skin.
My loved ones will be the death of me.
I burn in the middle of fire and love is hell to me.
For I am not invincible.
You do not know my thoughts at all,
You see beauty in all she is.
Sculptured by alabaster, marble and black granite.

I am a glass statue.
When moved I break,
Shards unrepairable on the ground.
In lights reflection I am shining brilliantly and patterned.
Yet how fragile I am.
I am not invincible.

I let you go so I can protect what is left of me.
It is sad and lonely,
But life is what it is
And I am what I am.

Like A Flower

Like a flower I feel it withering away,
My heart that is.
I felt it wilt, I felt it dry up,
There is nothing I can do to save it.
Petal by petal it is falling away,
By choices I have made or others made for me.
I can feel it die and I am helpless to save it.
I have laboured for it.
Watering it with logic,
Pruning it with faith,
Facing it in the sun of hope
But it is withering away.
It was strong once when it was part of a bush.
How it unrooted itself following broken dreams and
Worthless fantasies.
Now it is dying alone,
Falling on the path.
I watch it being trampled on the ground.
I kneel besides it with my head bowed down, tears falling.
I am helpless to save it.

Greatness

We heard them teach us from since childhood,
'We are destined for great things.'
Building blocks and toy cars for the boys,
Baby dolls with their houses and fairy tales for the girls.
They sent messages them toys to us since young.
Be millionaires own houses and buildings to the boys,
Marry well have thousands of babies in pink and blue to the girls.
They taught us nothing is impossible at school,
Believe it dream it work at it and you will be it.
Nothing wrong with selling dreams to children,
But reality kicked in quicker than we were prepared.
School got harder excelling became a challenge
Despite the effort.
This is when we first disappointed our parents.
Wishing stars refused to work,
How foolish we felt learning not all can
Be astronauts and Presidents only a handful.
Awaiting hubby with gold when you are well educated,
One cannot be silently humble.
No man I know respects witless fools.
So we entered adolescence not grown or young but awkward.
With life's first lessons.
School only got harder.
Some excelled, some fell out , others dropped out.
More parental disappointed faces less results.
Real life prince charming are presumptuous pretty boys,
Using you like a test tube for experiments.

Then came drugs, alcohol, sex and pregnancies.
Some made it out of high school alive knowing one or two who failed.
So much for greatness.
Life only got harder as we got older.
Privilege brought jobs for the one percenters.
Others started from the bottom till their up.
I know many who stayed at the bottom.
I close my eyes and think.
From astronauts,to Presidents,to doctors or lawyers.
Many had potential, what did they do with it?
What did I do with mine?
In a generation of racism, fighting sexism,
And most suicides from jobless youths where did we go wrong?
We were destined for greatness.
We went out seeking glory,
One or two found it.
I recall or at least this is what I think.
Greatness is truth.
The truth is greatness begun at birth.
To be who we are not kings not queens.
But they taught us lies and we aimed too high.
Now disappointed youths cut lives short,
The conceited steal and rob.
I wish they told me to be the best version of I alone,
Maybe I could sincerely smile now and then.

Do You Hear Me

If you only stopped and listened,
You would hear not just an echo.
Alas, tis not completely you at fault.
They taught you not to listen
As they tried to tame my wild spirit.
They loved and hated me altogether.
Married and disregarded me.
I was captured by soldiers and shared as a trophy,
When wars ended throughout history.
They forced and threatened me to silence with Death.
They called me love and beat me up remorselessly,
Making me property a piece of furniture.
Threatened me with violence should I make a sound.
But I scream regardless.
I will be heard.
I will endure for I am a fighter.
I shall always put up a fight,
For no daughter of mine will be born to injustice.
I hate no man truly speaking.
I love them all.
No words can describe what they are to me.
But I fight them for their ears.
So they hear my struggles,
Learn from my pain,
And right the wrongs created by their fore fathers.
So stop and listen for the echoes grow louder
And will soon become a voice of a billion if you don't listen.

I will be heard, I will be heard.
I may not be a lion but I am a lioness.
I am woman now hear me roar.

The One I Love The Most

I was searching for the one I would love the most.
I walked ends of the world.
Fell foolishly for the wrong ones,
While rejecting the right ones.
I was waiting for the one I would love the most.
I never found him.
Time went by they said I was coming of age.
Some said I was already of age.
Others insisted l was going to be too old if not careful.
Some argued I was to young to be anxious.
I was left confused if I ever wanted to marry soon.
Part of me wanted to be free,
Another wanted to be love ,
But mostly was afraid of loneliness.
So I was left half doubting, half wanting, half not wanting.
The one I would love the most I never found him
They say we all need someone.
They say times have changed you are your own love.
I was left confused by logic versus heart.
Reason versus emotion.
Till I found her one day.
The one I would love the most.
I realized without her I cannot be lovable or faithful.
Even God who I love unconditionally
Became distant as I tried to reach Him without her.
All I needed was to love her inside out.
Beauty and flaws,

Mistakes and achievements.
The one I was hoping to meet was here all along.
She is me.

Glory

We chase it we want it.
To be remembered as mighty is what we want.
Our weaknesses forgotten is what we want.
Have failures overcast by success is what we dream of.
Voices in our heads they suffered us,
We believed them truly.
Now we break our backs digging deeper into the grounds,
Seeking gold.
Breaking our skulls when we fall after attempting to fly,
Reaching for the skies.
Chasing mishaps.
Fighting for a seat at the table,
We will be one of the Big Boys.
Dying with our pain,
Humiliation must be remembered.
Motivated to keep running the finish line is getting closer
We never surrender we will show them.
Them who planted the voices in our mind,
Who called us nothing just to hurt us
It hurt , no it tormented us day by day.
For now we fear mistakes.
It proves them right, it proves them right.
So we labour till we sweat blood,
We think ourselves to madness.
Till we prove ourselves right.
Till we make ourselves proud,
For only then do the broken become fixed,

The restless sleep at night without tossing and turning,
The fighters put their weapons down.
Only when we have found it,
Only when the whole world sees it,
Us at the finish line,
Wearing a champion's medal,
Seating on an emperor's throne,
Knowing we have done it.
Only then do we smile a smile we mean.
When you see us in all our glory.

I Lie

I say I don't feel the need to be chosen first.
I lie.
No one wants to be picked last.
You are never picked last only taken
Without choice.
But I lie I do not care.
Of course I do.
Favoritism always roots insecurities.
Do I let you know how I feel?
Of course not.
I Lie.
I cannot have you see it bothers me the most
That I am always second choice.
How it hurts the feeling of not being good enough.
It keeps me up at night.
Should you know you would laugh and that will
Be the end of me.
So I lie.
I have always lied.
Even to myself.
For it hurts to admit the truth.
I was never second or last not even an option.
What is wrong with me.

Looking At Me

He saw me when no one did.
He loved what he saw,
All flaws I despised possessing
But I never knew he was looking at me.

He walked to the moon and back
To prove his worth.
Spoke from the heart how much he loved.
I took him to be like the others
Different skin same soul.
Looking for something that isn't love.
For I never knew he was looking at me.
Now I know but it is too late.
The ship has sailed.
So I am taking all the memories
And burying them faraway
Where I will never find them.
For I don't want to remember the way he looked at me.

Untitled

Lightning never strikes twice,
Once bitten twice shy.
Once was a mistake the second a coincidence
Third is recklessness.
Yet I am repeating the same story with a different man.

I thought he was different,
Hoped it would be different.
He gave it to me his heart and I took it into my careful arms.
Swearing an oath to guard it,
Vowed to care for it.
I never let it go and nursed it in my hands.
I thought I saw it grow
But I never noticed it wasn't thriving.
It starved.
Sad and lonely it began to shrink.
So small it slipped through the cracks of my hands and fell
Into a thousand pieces
But I took it for granted for I always had it
So I did not notice when it fell before me on the floor.
I stepped on whatever was left of it.
Only when it was too late I saw what I had done.
I wish I hadn't.
I am begging forgiveness.
But if you won't give it I can't say that I blame you,
For I haven't forgiven myself.

The Destroyer

They are those kind of people.
People like me.
Golden to the sight,
Perfection of beauty itself.
Turn heads when we walk,
Loved by many when we talk.
Behind sense of humor we hide.
The truth cannot be revealed.
We never feel as lovely as we look,
Or understand why we are loved
For we don't love ourselves.
So we break many a heart.
Unintentionally of course.
Our touch is not as golden as it seems.
More like iron grip.
Practically crushing your knuckles.
We break hearts for it is what we do best.
Hideous mess in the inside.
Monsters birth monstrosity.
Even when we love you the most,
We will destroy you.
Break your bones to nothing.
Unintentionally of course.
It is what we do best.

The Bitter Pill

It is hard to swallow,
As if your throat is not shallow,
Yet leaves you feeling shallow.
Life throws it's own version of truth,
Why then are you not satisfied and it feels falsified?
Prejudiced against you?
No really, is it you against the world?
But know this,
The world was before you were,
It will be there when you are no more.
It still is laughing and rejoicing while you weep.

Dreamers' Problem

Dreamers dream for its what we do best,
World becomes better when you envision possibility of paradise.
People speak their thoughts
When you give them a voice.
The world is complete when no soul is left behind.
There, there I said it.
Such a problem we writers have
Wishing to ease the pain of broken lives
Hoping to open the eyes of those who care less.
We write what we dream and dream we do
Songs we write for an audience
So as to change someone out there who listens
Impact those who understand.
Such a problem for dreamers this ambition is
For reality and dreams rarely marry.

Tomorrow

Tomorrow I promise shall be anew.
Years of yesterday shall be stories of years to come.
Struggles of today will be history
Written of how I came to be.
For we all begin somewhere.
Where years of slaves were shade
A hero was born for their salvation.
Where a loved one has left eternally
Another is born to calm the storm of misfortune.
Where a man searches peace
God finds him and calms his spirit.
So I cry today
I lash out my anger ballistic as middle
So tomorrow I will be silent as stove.
Tomorrow I will smile
Tomorrow I will be a legend.

Untitled

Broken promises are daggers to the heart.
Betray kills trust of those we love the most.
Friend becomes foe.
Springs have transformed into pits of fire.
Resentment grows as fondness fades away.
To love humans becomes a tragedy impossible.

Your Keeper

Through sands of time and ehoes of age,
We heard them sing the very same song.
'My broken heart, poor broken abused heart.'
I saw it for myself in the lives of others.
Not me said I.
So I took my complete naïve beating heart,
Shackled it to prevent from straying,
Caged it as precaution to flying,
Built a fortress with walls so high
No heartbreaker could ever catch a glimpse.
Stay here chained, inexpierenced untamed romatic.
Keep put in this cage, curious trusting one.
Behind these walls you are safe from wolves, poor easy prey.
Don't cry for freedom my sad lonely heart,
You will end in pieces beyond repair.
Trust me to keep you safe for I am your keeper.

The Foe Who Is Never A Friend

By my name I bring nightmares to those who hear it.
My voice echies tragedy to those who listen.
I struggle to fight my imsge of a foe.
Persevering in pain to become a friend.
Alas, my efforts are unfruitful.
In your eyes I resemble Death.
I pray today is when I become loved.
I smile think positive
Yet again like a fool I am treated.
So I weep like a widow who has lost it all.
To them I am nothing but an annoyance.
Wht do I fight to be seen?
Hope to be loved?
Cry to be cherished?
Do I really need anyone?

Passing

Ashes to ashes another goes,
Far from reach,
Unseen unheard forever no more.
Another disappears into oblivion,
A memory they become,
Reduced to a statistic.
For none are immortal,
We live to die,
And the legacy remains.
Gone are the giants.

# The Dreamer

Time spent in my thoughts
Of what will become.
I chase the impossible hoping for possibility.
I believe in wishes,
Fighting for all to come true
One day I will finish at the peak of the mountain.

There are moments those moments,
Doubt screams in my head,
I wonder what is to become?
I stumble I fall,
Broken flat on my face.
I remember such is life,
Reality and dreams enemies forever.
Bruised and battered I arise
From where I left off.
I have heard of dreamers become giants.
They lost yet never gave up.
Perseverance a mighty word.
I have never seen a giant.
Ywt stories of their journey have become stuff of legend.
Some legends are made,
Some giants are born,
Yet all are determined.

Untitled

The light begins to dim.
Another fruitless dream,
I fight and hold back tears
Yet one can not deny the pain of
Another wasted journey.
Efforts die in vain.
The light that burnt like fire,
Fire of future love and hope
Is all but a low flicker now.
A candle in the dark.
I sit still lost in thoughts
As the wax melts away.
What now? Where to? Then what?
I think I plot I struggle.
All this time I saw where I was headed
Today change has knocked on my door
Left me in a house of sorrow.
And a candle alone to last the night.
The future I saw is now darkness.
I will never see the light.

Questions

They call it a test.
If so,
When will I pass?
Or perharps fail?
When will it end?
Life's never ending struggles.
They call it life,
It drives me insane.
Sometimes I converse with myself in my mind
Or say it out loud for the universe to hear.
Of course it makes no sense.
For I am going mad.
Mad with sadness,
Mad with fear.
Is it wrongto want a little control?
Or am I destined to be the doomed?
No salvation for me then?
If so,
Let it all burn.
Here I go again driving myself crazy.
Who am I?
What am I?
Why am I here?

Looking Back

I hurt you didn't I?
I am sorry .
I do that a lot,
Hurt people
Including me.
I have always been strong
But strength is not kindness
And I have been unkind.
I have always been a savior
Focused on the goal and I refused destructions.
I know now as I see it clearly
All that I have done.
None to be proud of.
I hurt you
I hurt people
Including me.
I hate myself for it.
I can never forgive myself for this .
I am breaking down.
I am falling apart.

Ambitious

I look up
High and up.
The sky is the limit
Keep on going.
Mountains in sight,
A mere obstacle.
Voices of doubt,
A minor annoyance.
I am determined
I am tomorrow
I am the future
No one could be greater.
I will carve my name into earth's core
Stars will never shine brighter
History will remember
I will be larger than giants
They will call me 'impossible.'

The Raven

She is dark and strong
Ungraceful and strange.
She is not a dove pure in beauty
She is different.
The big strong black bird.
She is unwelcomed
Sign of tragedy.
She is a hunter never a pet.
She is free yet flies alone.
She is blackbird in the skies alone.
Her song is a different melodt.
Nor sweat as a robin's
Not powerdul like an eagle's.
It is a loud shriek mistaken for irritation
The tragic blackbird a creature of sorrow.
The beautiful blackbird.

The Last Resort

When all else fails with nothing left to lose,
Choices have narrowed to less than a narrow bridge,
With the last option longer than longer than one.
With a brave face and forced smile
Taking whatever is left for the taking,
Whatever crumbs fallen from the table,
Picking up dust and storing in a bag
For there always cones a time
One has nothing left to do.

The Night

You walk alone in an empty street.
Darkest is the night
Doors are closed to your aid.
Street lights are your only company.
You are cold and numb
Hungry and weak.
Your heartaches as tears sting your eyes.
You hold back tears
You keep walking.
Walking down the lonely empty street.
Theives will come and rob
Muggers will do the same
For evening is the time for killers.
You feel it feeding your soul with fear
You want to cry out for tomorrow.
Tomorrow comes in daybreak.
The bodyguard you prayed for.
Nothing to fear you are stronger than you know.

About the Author

Tanyaradzwa Vimbai Mombeshora is a amauter lover of history and literature and has studied journalism and communication. She also has poetry books published and songwriting in works.